Telephones Over the Years

by S. J. Brown

Scott Foresman
is an imprint of

Glenview, Illinois • Boston, Massachusetts • Chandler, Arizona
Upper Saddle River, New Jersey

Photographs

Every effort has been made to secure permission and provide appropriate credit for photographic material. The publisher deeply regrets any omission and pledges to correct errors called to its attention in subsequent editions.

Unless otherwise acknowledged, all photographs are the property of Pearson Education, Inc.

Photo locators denoted as follows: Top (T), Center (C), Bottom (B), Left (L), Right (R), Background (Bkgd)

ISBN 13: 978-0-328-50800-6
ISBN 10:   0-328-50800-4

When you want to talk to someone who is far away, what do you do? Most likely, you pick up your telephone and make a call. These days you can call almost anybody anywhere in the world. You just push a few buttons. As you are about to learn, things were not always like that.

Boston

New York

In 1883, phone wires were put up between New York City and Boston. Then the people in these two cities could talk to each other.

The first telephone was built by the **inventor** Alexander Bell in 1876. It used electricity to send people's voices over wires. Until then, there was no way to talk to someone in a different place.

Once the phone was invented, it didn't take long for people to want one. The first city to ever have a telephone **system** was New Haven, Connecticut. That was in 1877, only a year after the phone was invented. Other cities soon built telephone systems, as well.

It would take just a few more years before people in different cities could also talk to each other.

Then, phone wires were strung across the country. People in New York could talk to someone all the way in California. By 1927, you could call someone on the other side of the Atlantic Ocean! It took weeks for a boat to travel from New York to London, England, but someone in New York could call and talk to a friend in London in less than a minute.

By 1927, someone in London, England, could call a friend who was in New York City.

London

New York

As the years went by, more and more places got telephone systems. Different kinds of **technology** were used to connect the systems. These days, almost everyone is just a phone call away.

New York

Seattle

Sao Paolo

Before telephones, it could take weeks or even months to communicate with friends and family in distant places. Now people who live far away can talk to each other. They can share what is happening in their lives much more easily. Is there anyone you like to call who lives far away?

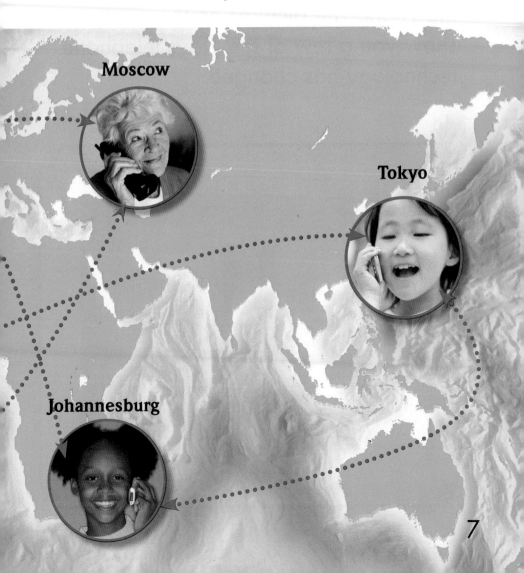

Moscow

Tokyo

Johannesburg

Take a look at the picture below. Can you guess what it is? If you guessed a telephone, then you are right.

This is a picture of the first telephone. It was built by Alexander Graham Bell in 1876. It is probably much different from the phone in your house.

Telephones have changed a lot over the years. The pictures on these pages show you a few of the ways telephone technology has changed.

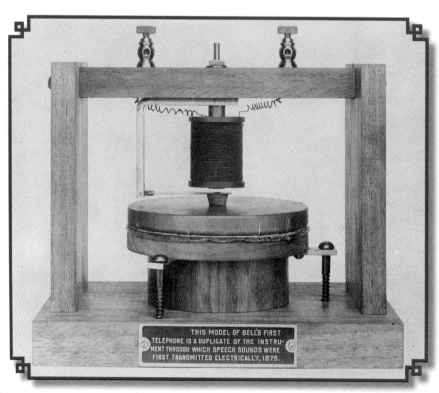

THIS MODEL OF BELL'S FIRST TELEPHONE IS A DUPLICATE OF THE INSTRUMENT THROUGH WHICH SPEECH SOUNDS WERE FIRST TRANSMITTED ELECTRICALLY, 1875.

This is the first phone that people could buy and use. People talked and listened using the same part of the phone. The part you listen at is called the receiver. The part you talk into is called the mouthpiece.

1877

This telephone hung on the wall. On this phone the mouthpiece and the receiver are in different places.

Receiver

Mouthpiece

Mouthpiece

By 1930, phones were smaller and easier to use.

1882

Receiver

1930

Look at these phones. What do you think of them? Notice that none of them have numbers that you can push or dial. So, how did they work? Let's find out.

9

This person is calling the operator.

The operator uses a switchboard to put the call through. The switchboard allows your phone line to connect to other people's phone lines.

With early phones, you would not dial a number yourself. You picked up the receiver of your telephone and an operator would answer. The operator asked whom you were trying to reach. The operator then used special equipment to call that person for you.

The pictures on these pages show you the steps that were needed to make a phone call.

In 1880, a man named Almon Strowger from Kansas City, Missouri, decided he didn't like the idea of using telephone operators. He thought that

The phone rings at the place you are trying to reach.

the operators were giving the wrong people his telephone calls. He was **determined** to do something about it. So he invented an **automatic** phone system. With his system, a caller could dial numbers and call someone directly. People no longer needed to go through an operator.

By 1924, many people used Strowger's system instead of using operators.

This was a Strowger phone. It was made in the late 1890s. Unlike earlier phones, this phone has a dial with numbers on it.

This kind of phone was first made in the 1940s. You can still find people using them today.

This unusually shaped phone was first made in the early 1960s.

This phone is called a cordless phone. People started using it in the 1980s. This kind of phone lets people move around while they talk.

In the early 1960s there was another big change in telephones. Now, instead of dialing a number, you could push numbered buttons.

As time went on, phones continued to change. Look at the phones on this page. Have you seen these kinds of phones?

The very first cell phone was made in 1973. As time went on cell phones became much smaller and more popular. Some cell phones now let you take and send pictures to people who are far away.

As you can see, telephones—and the way we use them—have changed a lot since the days of Alexander Bell. Most likely, new kinds of telephones and new ways to use them will be invented in the future. Do you have any ideas about new telephones in the future? Perhaps you will invent one someday.

Now Try This

Phones of the Future

You've just learned a lot about how phones have changed over the past years. Now it's time to think about the future.

You and a partner are going to design a phone of the future. Before you and a partner begin, take some time to talk about what your phone will be like. What do you want your phone to do? Would you like to wear your phone like a ring or perhaps a watch? Your phone can do anything you want it to do— even watch a movie. Follow the steps on page 15.

1. Think about what your phone will look like. What shape is it? What color should it be?
2. Remember, you can make your phone look like anything you want. You can even make it look like a toy or doll.
3. Work with your partner to make a drawing of your telephone.
4. Label the different parts and what they do.
5. Under your drawing, name your phone and tell why it is special.
6. When you are done, share your new phone invention with the rest of the class.

Glossary

automatic *adj.* something that works by itself

determined *adj.* having one's mind made up

inventor *n.* someone who designs and creates new, useful things

system *n.* a group of things that work together

technology *n.* the use of science to improve or make something